"God's Answer to Anxiety and Fear is a helpful tool for pastors and church planters as they deal with stress in their own lives or in the lives of those they minister to. I found the lessons to be simple yet deep in content. The READ/REFLECT/JOURNAL/PRAY/ACT approach gives the reader the ability to interact with the text and to implement the lessons being taught. This is a book that one could go through annually, and then compare journal notes from the previous year." - Dr. Gary Teja

Dr. Gary Teja is the Director of Global Strategic Initiatives for Multiplication Network. He has over 40 years of experience at Christian Reformed World Missions (CRWM), now known as Resonate Global, CRC Publications, Christian Reformed Home Missions, Kuyper College, and Bible League International. Gary has written over 30 publications.

"In giving hope to those who deal with anxiety and fear, Wally demonstrates his pastoral heart. He lays out the importance of knowing God through faith in Jesus Christ. He consistently points us to the character of our God - his attributes of love, grace, and faithfulness. I also appreciate how well he integrates readings, prayers, journaling, and specific action steps for each day. As he writes, "This is more than just a devotional. It's a program." In my opinion, it's a very effective program, and I highly recommend it. In the words of a beautiful song, "I am no longer a slave to fear. I am a child of God" - Pastor Jeff Dykema

Jeff Dykema is a retired pastor of 28 years from Sunshine Community Church in El Paso, Texas. He has served on the boards of World Missions and Calvin University. He currently serves on the board of All Nations Seminary in Juarez, Mexico, and on the board of Pregnancy and Fatherhood Solutions in El Paso.

God's Answer for Anxiety and Fear

A DAILY PROGRAM TO BRING YOU CLOSER TO PEACE IN YOUR LIFE.

Wally De La Fuente

Published By:
Osvaldo De La Fuente Jr.
5600 Harvey Street. Suite 1046
Muskegon, MI 49444
United States
www.wallydelafuente.com

GOD'S ANSWER FOR ANXIETY AND FEAR
A Daily Program to Bring You Closer to Peace In Your Life

PRINTED IN THE UNITED STATES OF AMERICA

Cover artwork by HMD Publishing
Layout design by HMD Publishing

First Printing Edition, June 2023
ISBN: 9798375847436

For my brother Joseph,

*I know anxiety has been a factor in your life, but you are overcoming it!
Whenever you feel fear, anxiety, or worry, this book is here to remind
you that God is the answer. The Bible holds the key to your peace.*

PREFACE

Always Seek Help

Upon completing this book, I gave it to some trusted pastors and mentors to read. I was delighted to know they enjoyed the book, thought it was useful and had great things to say about the format (read, reflect, journal, pray, act). One of these trusted mentors came back to me with some very important suggestions. This is what he wrote.

“*Like the format and words of encouragement given throughout each chapter. The Bible passages selected are very appropriate for those struggling with anxiety and fear. The prayer suggestions are very meaningful and the suggested actions help the reader implement the instructions being given. If I had one suggestion based on my experience of interactions with Christ followers over 48 years of ministry, there have been discoveries in the medical world that, for a small percentage of the population, there is within their DNA a natural predisposition to being overly anxious and fearful. Some of these people are confessing Christians who may live with guilt and they need reassurance, I believe, that God completely understands and does not see them as less a Christian than those who do not struggle with anxiety and fear issues. I know people who have received counseling and medicine (medicine, by the way, I have to believe God in His Sovereignty has permitted to be created) to assist them with their struggle and has proven helpful. I think it important to acknowledge there are some Christians who, even though they would follow everything you write about in this book, will still struggle with some anxiety and fear all because it is in their genetic makeup. These Christians, rather than to be given more guilt and anxiety, need to receive encouragement to seek the services of a reputable Christian counselor and, if necessary, the help from their primary physician that certain medicines can provide for them."* - Pastor Jack Doorlag

Pastor Jack is right. This book is inended to help those who are seeking a spritual journey into discoverying the answers to freedom from anxiety and fear from God and His Holy Bible. It will give them valuable advice from God's word and how to apply it to their lives to become closer to a life without worry or fear.

But there will be those of you who will need to find professional help and should do so. If you do seek professional help, this book is still an amazing companion to help change your mindset on what you are going through mentally and physically. It will motivate you to examine the way you think about fear and anxiety and change the way you act and react to possible outside triggers that cause you to feel this way.

If you need outside help, know that there is no shame in that. God still loves you and wants you to be free. You are still His child and He will not leave you nor forsake you. This fear and anxiety you feel is not the part of the person God intended you to be. As a child of God, you are no longer the person who lives in fear and anxiety. That person is dead. You may not feel that way now but it is part of having faith. Have faith in God He is transforming you into what you are intended to be.

"I have been crucified with Christ; it is no longer I who live, but Christ lives in me; and the life which I now live in the flesh I live by faith in the Son of God, who loved me and gave Himself for me."
Galatians 2:20

If you find you are still struggling by the end of this book, please seek further help. You can always come back to this book to help you along the way. You live in this flesh who fears and feels anxious but you also live by faith in the Son of God because He died and gave Himself up for you so you can live in freedom.

Contents

DAY ONE
Anxiety & Fear......6

DAY TWO
The Program......16

DAY THREE
A Matter Of The Heart......22

DAY FOUR
I Am Your God......30

DAY FIVE
Don't Worry About Anything......36

DAY SIX
My Peace, I Give You......42

DAY SEVEN
God's Perfect Love......48

DAY EIGHT
Being Perfected In Love......52

DAY NINE
Trusting His Faithfulness......58

DAY TEN
Could Anxiety Be A Blessing?......64

DAY ELEVEN
Gratefulness Drives Out Worry......68

DAY TWELVE
Fighting Fear When You've Made A Mess......72

DAY THIRTEEN
Fighting Fear When You Didn't Make The Mess......78

DAY FOURTEEN
He Is With You In The Valley 84

DAY FIFTEEN
He Cares For You 90

DAY SIXTEEN
Specific Prayers For Specific Worries 96

DAY SEVENTEEN
Receiving God's Work In You 100

DAY EIGHTEEN
All Things For Good 104

DAY NINETEEN
God Is Dependable 108

DAY TWENTY
Resting In His Presence 114

DAY TWENTY-ONE
Never Alone 118

DAY TWENTY-TWO
Anxiety Is A Liar 124

DAY TWENTY-THREE
Trusting In God To Change You 128

DAY TWENTY-FOUR
It's A Process 134

DAY ONE

Anxiety & Fear

As a child I struggled with quite a bit of anxiety. It didn't matter if the situations were major or minor, I would have an "attack." The feeling of being left out was a major one to deal with. When I was younger, I disliked missing school because I always felt as though I would miss out on something important. The fear of missing out resulted in crazy dreams haunting me at night.

I once dreamt I was at home with a cold. I tried to get to school because I felt I was going to miss something. Something important. After finally pleading with my mother, I ran out the door and up the street to the school. I hopped over the rock wall fencing and noticed something immediately; footprints. There were footprints like that of the poem along the dirt yard leading into the school.

I followed them as fast as I could into the school. I raced up and down the empty hallways searching for anyone. But everyone was gone! As I made my way back outside, I saw the steps again. This time there were so many more! Many children began running, and as I looked up, I saw Jesus in the distance. He was standing in the middle of the yard as the last child lifted into the air. He turned to me from a far, put His head down in sadness, and looked back up into the sky. He was then lifted away into the clouds and was gone. I missed it… I was left behind! Imagine dreaming that as a 12-year-old!

I've also battled anxiety with little things like tickling. I can't stand to be tickled! As a child, whenever someone tickled me, I had the sensation that I was going to run out of breath and die! Now, when my wife tries to tickle me, she may be the victim of an unconscious response like an elbow or a kick. I have a very knee-jerk reaction to the whole thing. Needless to say, she doesn't tickle me at all.

Of course, I have other anxieties now that I'm older. How will I support my family? Will I make the next deadline on time? What will people think of me? When will I be able to retire? Will my children still love me in the future? And, heaven forbid, what if I forget my phone at home?!

There are so many reasons to be anxious. We live in an anxiety-prone world. Far more people than you can imagine are struggling with this and being challenged by it every day. Statistics show that anxiety and fear in people seem to be growing every year. As of the time of writing this book, there has been a noticeable increase in the suicide rate and the prevalence of illnesses caused by stress and anxiety over the past two years.

Anxiety and fear are two of the most misunderstood afflictions that exist. They sometimes co-exist and are often mistaken for each other. But there is a difference. We will discuss the differences later, but you may find it interesting that God commands us to never fear and never be anxious. You may be asking yourself, "How am I supposed to do that?" How are you supposed to "stop" living in fear and anxiety?

You often feel weighed down with anxiety and worry. It feels like constantly leaning back in your chair, almost tipping over, but managing to catch yourself just in time…. all day long! You may have even given up the possibility of a stable, radiant, confident, courageous, astoundingly fruitful life because you've lived in fear for so long.

We have all been afraid, but fear puts us in a self-made hell. It can control our lives, steal our sleep, destroy our relationships, and generally makes us miserable prisoners in our own minds and bodies.

"Research indicates that individuals with anxiety disorders may be at a higher risk for developing various chronic medical conditions. They may also have more severe symptoms and a greater risk of death when they become ill," according to Harvard Health.

Some of the common medical problems that may be related to anxiety include:

- Respiratory Conditions, such as asthma and COPD

- Gastrointestinal Conditions, such as IBS and ulcers

- Heart Disease

- Substance abuse and addiction

- Migraines

You may feel alone, but you're not!

Anxiety Disorders affect 18.1% of adults in the United States (approximately 40 million adults between the ages of 18 to 54) - National Institute of Mental Health (NIMH). Apr 25, 2017.

Although anxiety is very treatable, only 36% of those with anxiety seek treatment.

However, people with anxiety are 3-5 times more likely to seek medical treatment and 6 times more likely to be hospitalized for psychiatric illness than those who do not have anxiety.

The impact of anxiety can range from mild to severe, from tiresome to devastating. Some forms of anxiety require serious intervention from professionals, often involving medication. Please consult a medical professional if you're struggling with the devastating effects of anxiety.

Most people recognize that worry of any variety takes a toll on their mental wellbeing. Fewer people are aware of the *physical* side effects. In the short term, our body's natural response to stress is not harmful — adrenaline, increased heart rate, and blood flow help us to focus on a problem and constructively deal with it.

Prolonged stress, even if it stems from typical daily challenges, can have negative effects on one's physical and mental health.

Common situations such as apprehension about traffic, missing a deadline, meetings you're not quite prepared for, interviews, crying children, and more responsibilities than you can fit in — can trigger a physical response due to apprehension or anxiety.

There are also much broader categories:

- Money and job security
- The future
- Health
- Children
- School

That's just the short list of topics we are always tempted to be anxious about!

Many of the things we worry about are small things, while others are significant. Some worries are rational, while others are in the irrational category. Anxiety can sometimes manifest as excessive worry, to the point where one may become concerned about whether they are worrying too much.

This may or may not comfort you, but dealing with anxiety is a part of life. As long as we exist in this world, the temptation to feel anxious will remain close at hand.

The world offers a myriad of practical suggestions for battling anxiety — exercise, getting more sleep, support groups, individual counseling, therapy, and many others.

While these concepts may be helpful to some extent and there is no reason not to adopt those that you find particularly beneficial; it is far more helpful to recognize that there is One who has conquered anxiety and fear on your behalf.

Because of God's immense love for us, He shares with us how to experience peace despite our anxious thoughts. In the Bible, we can find God's answer for fear and anxiety!

Anxiety and fear can take years away from us, ruin our memories, overwhelm our lives, and make us wish we were never born. They can destroy the lives God designed us to have.

What is the difference between anxiety and fear?

The answer is simpler than you think.

"There's a distinct, key difference between fear and anxiety. Fear results from a clear and present danger, while anxiety results from the anticipation of an unspecified threat." Talk Space Mental Health Conditions

In other words, fear is an uncontrollable emotion that is there to protect us from real danger. When you walk in the woods and spot a bear, you fear. You fear for your life. Your body goes into fight or flight mode because fear is trying to protect you. See the following list from Talk Space.

(https://www.talkspace.com/mental-health/conditions/articles/fear-vs-anxiety/)

Physiological symptoms of fear:

- Quick, shallow breathing
- Shortness of breath
- Hot flashes or chills
- Rapid heartbeat
- Upset stomach
- Goosebumps
- Tight chest
- Dry mouth
- Trembling
- Sweating
- Nausea

Psychological symptoms of fear:

- Feeling detached from your body
- Inability to focus and concentrate

- Feeling a sense of stress
- Lacking emotional control
- A pending sense of doom

Physical symptoms of fear:

- Flight response (running for safety)
- Freezing up (inability to move)
- Displaying violence
- Clenching fists

On the other hand, anxiety is believing you could be attacked by a bear while walking in the woods. Nonetheless, there are no bears within miles of your location. You are putting your mind and body through the process of fear without ever being in danger in the first place.

Physiological symptoms of anxiety:

- Trembling or shaking
- Sweating
- Tightness in the chest area
- Upset stomach and nausea
- Quick, shallow breathing
- Chills or hot flashes
- Rapid heart rate
- Muscle pain
- Headaches
- Dizziness

Psychological symptoms of anxiety:

- Inability to focus on conversations, tasks, or thoughts

- Racing, negative thoughts
- Sense of impending doom
- Feeling overwhelmed
- Constant worrying
- Catastrophizing
- Restlessness
- Irritability
- Fatigue

Physical symptoms of anxiety:

- Inability to complete mundane tasks
- Difficulty sitting still and staying calm
- Drug and alcohol use
- Being startled easily
- Social withdrawal

There is a way to be free from fear and anxiety on this side of heaven! God does not want His children to live in fear or be paralyzed by anxiety. He offers you a life of joy, confidence, contentment, stability, and fruitfulness. In short, He offers you an abundant life.

Pray

Every day you will see a prayer just like the one you see below. Read it out loud as a prayer to God. You can add more by just talking to God. God is ready to listen and help you as you have needs. Don't be afraid to reach out to Him daily! The Bible says, *"Draw near to God, and He will draw near to you."* James 4:8

Lord, help me learn more about how I can be free from anxiety and fear in my life. Show me from your Word (the Bible) all your promises, commands, counsel, and comfort. I have committed to learning what you have to say about how I feel and how I can be healed from it. Heal me as I go through this program, in Jesus' name.

Journal

You may use the space provided, but it may be best to use your own journal.

- Did you know there were Bible verses that talk about anxiety and fear? If so, which can you remember?

Act

- Go to your Bible or a website like biblegateway.com or bible. com and search for the word *"fear."* How many did you find? What about the word *"anxiety?"*

DAY TWO

The Program

This is more than just a devotional. It's a program.

In case you are not familiar with one, a devotional is a specific spiritual reading for each day. To actively and effectively engage in daily devotional practice, you read the Bible verse and the specific text, reflect on the accompanying thought or teaching, and spend some time in prayer. It is a great way to experience the Bible daily. The issue occurs when there is no change in your life because you don't take any action. You don't take the necessary steps to apply it to your life and make a change.

This is more like a **daily program**. You will read the Bible, reflect on the chapter, and pray, BUT you will also have to journal and take specific actions and steps in your life to get closer to being free!

Ways to use this book

1. **Use this book as a group**. You can use this book to guide others to freedom from fear and anxiety in a group setting. Each can take the daily steps, and then you can all get together once a week or at a set time and discuss what you learned, what changes are happening in your life, and what wins are taking place in your journey to freedom! There is a wonderful sense of not being alone when you take the time to take a journey with others.

2. **Use this book with a trusted partner.** Maybe a group is too much. Maybe your anxiety comes from working in a group! But you do have a trusted friend. One that will go through this book with you, hold you accountable for change, and/or be there

for you when you become overwhelmed. Having a partner makes everything easier and a lot less scary.

3. **Use this book on your own.** It's okay to do this on your own. The fact is you are not alone. You are going through this book with God on your side. He has been there the whole time. Take the time to read, pray, journal and take action, knowing that God is with you the entire way!

Are you ready to get started? Are you ready to finally take steps towards a life free from fear and anxiety? If you are, the journey begins tomorrow.

Prepare yourself!

This is going to be a lifestyle-changing journey. To really experience it, you will have to create new habits. Creating new habits also creates outer obstacles and inner obstacles that will try to prevent you from reaching the end of the journey. You will want to quit before the program is over. Don't. The key is to look outside yourself and upward only to God in order to stay focused. There are a few other things you can do to help this journey become a reality in your life.

Time

Make sure you set a time every day to work on the program. It is best to set the same time every day. You can use this to replace your devotional time. Pick a time and do it every day at that time. Give yourself at least 15 minutes to work. Create a habit.

Place

Find a perfect place where you can be alone without distractions. A place where you feel at peace, free from anxiety, and free to learn. This could be an office, a bench in the park, or a living room. Just make sure you can be alone in this place for the time you will be there.

Tools

Make sure you have a notebook and your favorite writing utensil. Although there are placeholders in this book, you will want to take notes. Taking notes will commit the material to memory. You will be much more likely to retain the information. Keep a notepad or a journal. You will be asked to journal throughout the program.

Share

If you are working in a group, share your thoughts, parts of your journal, or questions. You can also share with a trusted friend or mentor. Sharing with someone will put you in the mindset of commitment and accountability.

What to expect

The way to get the most from this program is to read one chapter per day. Pray and journal each day. Do not try to go forward or do two chapters per day. Allow the content to simmer in your mind. Meditate on it throughout your day. If you miss a day, that's okay. Just pick up from where you left off when you come back.

Remember, for some of you; it has taken your whole life to get to this point with anxiety and fear. Take it one day at a time. But first, we pray!

Pray

Lord, help me on this journey. You know how I've struggled with fear and anxiety, and I believe you are the only cure that can set me free. Keep me focused and relying on you throughout this program. When I don't feel like putting in the work, remind me of the benefits of getting through it all. In Jesus' name. Amen.

Time to Journal

You may use the space provided, but it may be best to use your own journal.

- Is anxiety a consistent challenge in your life, or does it only arise occasionally? Explain how and when it does.

- Which remedies have you tried — either spiritual or practical — that have worked for you? Which ones have NOT worked?

Act

Take a piece of paper and write down your commitment to this process.

I am committed to completing this program because __________ (write your reason here). I will not give up. I will read and take action every day. When I finish this program, I__________ (write down what you will look like at the end of the program.

Now seal it up in an envelope, and we will open it at the end of the program. Will you commit yourself to this? Write it down now, seal it in an envelope, and put it in a safe place.

DAY THREE

A Matter Of The Heart

My wife and I had some dear friends over for Thanksgiving one year. He was a self-professed atheist at the time. We were discussing politics, family, and religion; all the last things people should not be talking about on Thanksgiving.

He said, "All religions are basically the same."

"Sure," I answered. "All except one."

Why am I telling you this story? For you to understand and utilize God's answer for fear and anxiety, you must first know God. You must first have a relationship with Him. Those who have a relationship with God are God's children. If you are already a child of God, you may skip this chapter and move on, although you may gain some wonderful knowledge if you stick with us. If you are not yet a child of God, please read on. This will change your entire life!

All Religions are the Same.

See, all religions *are* the same. Every single religion will require you to do something to get something.

Below are some examples of religions and their end goal to get rewarded:

Zoroastrianism - the person needs to win the struggle over evil.

Judaism - You must obey the Jewish law and customs.

Islam - Muslims must practice the five pillars successfully.

Hinduism - The individual must purify himself from evil in life and afterlife.

Sikhism - Proper worship and conduct must be performed in order to be worthy to be saved.

Confucianism - Heaven on earth is possible, but only through personal conformity to the rules of society.

Shintoism - Must maintain Japanese supremacy at all costs.

Buddhism - Must renounce self in order to reach Nirvana.

Taoism - Must maintain Yin/Yang balance; otherwise, no harmony.

Paganism - Must appease the gods and spirits in order to be rewarded.

Atheism - compliance to a system or a philosophy. You must comply to be happy, or practice total non-compliance in order to be free. So, you're either going to be an anarchist - break all the rules, or keep all the rules, but you've got to deal with the rules either way.

And all these claims lead to a certain type of "reward" or "freedom."

But in Christianity, we seek "salvation."

So, my friend was kind of right. To reach or attain whatever it is any religion is offering, a person needs to *DO* something. You must work to be saved.

So, I told him, "All religions **are** the same except for Christianity."

Todd Friel is the host of Wretched TV and Radio. In a discussion with another atheist on a college campus, he was told that the Bible is just like any other book from any other religion. Here is what he had to say.

"Here is what all of those other books say to do. Be good. Try hard. Potentially get rewarded. And that goes with every other system, I'll throw in Buddhism, I'll throw in Hinduism, I'll throw in Sikhism, I'll even

throw in modern-day Judaism. They all teach work. When you study Christianity, it has a unique and exclusive message. All of your righteous deeds are like filthy rags. Our good deeds are not good at all because they are offered from sin-stained hands and we can do nothing to appease God. We need a rescuer, and the Bible provides it in the person of Jesus Christ, who died for sinners. Not for good people, for sinners."

See, Christianity is the only belief system that gives you salvation as a free gift. There is no work to be done. In fact, if you try to earn salvation through Christianity, it is rejected and not Christianity at all. Furthermore, salvation in Christianity means salvation from sin and death. In other religions, it means self-enlightenment or to better yourself.

Christianity is based on the fact that we are all sinners. There is no way for us to earn our way into heaven because we are undeserving, unworthy, and sinful people.

The Bible says,

"For all have sinned and fall short of the glory of God" - Romans 3:23

No matter what we try to do, we can't reach God. We can't reach heaven. In fact, the Bible also states,

"For the wages of sin is death" - Romans 6:23

We are all sinners, and because we have that sinful nature in our lives, we are dead. Not only do we die physically, but we are dead spiritually. But God does not leave us abandoned.

"But God demonstrates his own love for us in this: While we were still sinners, Christ died for us." - Romans 5:8

He gave up His only Son as a substitute for our sins. Jesus died on the cross and rose again on the third day so that we could be saved. He conquered fear. He conquered sin. He conquered death. We didn't ask for it, and we don't have to work to get it.

"the gift of God is eternal life in Christ Jesus our Lord." - Romans 6:23

Why did God choose to give us eternal life in heaven with Him even though we are sinners?

"For God so loved the world that He gave His only begotten Son, that whoever believes in Him should not perish but have everlasting life."
John 3:16

Because He loved the world He created and everything in it. All we must *do* is believe it. It takes faith. It is hard to believe in something we can't see or touch or hear, but God is real even when we can't see Him. He is real and ready to be by your side through the rest of your life.

The Bible also says,

"He chose us in Him before the foundation of the world," Ephesians 1:4

God has thought of you since the beginning of time and specifically chose you to read this book at this very moment to understand the words you are currently reading. Why? So that you may believe.

Why is this important? Because, when you understand that God called you to be His child from the beginning of time, the One who created the Universe, then you will know that you are not alone. There is no reason to fear. No reason to be anxious. God is on your side!

So what is the next step?

"If you declare with your mouth, "Jesus is Lord," and believe in your heart that God raised him from the dead, you will be saved."
- Romans 10:9

So that's it! Speak the words right now. Tell God that Jesus is your Lord and Savior, and if you truly believe in your heart that God raised Him from the dead, you are saved!

"for everyone who calls on the name of the Lord will be saved."
Romans 10:13

Everyone. That includes you.

Believing in the Bible, that Jesus died for you, and that God loves you is crucial because it is the only way God's Answer for Fear and Anxiety will have an impact on your life. Do you believe it? If so, here is your first assignment.

Pray

The first step in believing is speaking it. Believing and speaking equal faith in a sense. Pray along with this prayer out loud…

Lord. I need you. I am a sinner and know that there is nothing I can do to be saved. You sent Your Son to die in my place so that I can be with You and have eternal life. I believe it with all my heart. Thank you for saving me from sin and death and more importantly, myself.

Time To Journal

It's imperative that we record important dates and times in our lives. Take a moment to fill in the blanks below.

- How did you feel before you prayed?

- How did you feel after you prayed?

- Today you became a child of God. Write down today's date.

- Remember, if we declare with our mouths that Jesus is Lord and that God raised Him from the dead, we are saved. Who will you declare it to? Who will you tell the good news to?

Act

Go and tell someone what just happened to you. Remember, you need to declare it with your mouth. Tell someone you trust. Perhaps someone who already believes in Jesus as well; but tell someone. Do you know what this makes you? A child of God. You can now enter a relationship with Him. You can now benefit from this book.

DAY FOUR

I Am Your God

Read: *"Fear not, for I am with you; Be not dismayed, for I am your God. I will strengthen you, Yes, I will help you, I will uphold you with My righteous right hand." Isaiah 41:10*

Reflect

As children of God, we have the privilege of knowing and having a personal relationship with the one true God. He is the one who has declared, *"I am your God"* (Isaiah 41:10), and it is in Him that we can find true security and comfort.

Perhaps more than anything else, God desires His children to have faith and trust in Him. Do we? Have we acted in such a way that shows He is worthy of our confidence? When we face various situations in life, it is essential to question whether we are genuinely depending on God to protect and lead us or if we are relying solely on our own strength and abilities. God's call to Israel in this text is the same one He makes to us. His abiding presence with us should be enough to banish all fear.

But this means we must know who He is.

He tells Israel not to fear "for *I* am with you...for *I* am your *God.*" Who is the "I"? "I" is the God who created the universe. "I" is the one who formed you in your mother's womb. "I" is the one who had a plan for your life before the world was ever created—the all-knowing, all-powerful, always everywhere God. Clearly, God expects that the promise of His presence would be enough to set His people free from fear. But that assumes they, and we, know who this constantly present One is.

This verse begins to explain some of His character and ability. He is the one who strengthens and helps us. He upholds us personally with His hand. He is not merely a passive bystander, but He personally and actively infuses us with enablement, assistance, and overshadowing protection.

The larger context of the verse elaborates on what God can do for His people. He equips them for victory in battle (vv. 11-16) and supernaturally meets their needs (vv. 17-20). His power turned towards the benefit and blessing of His people, coupled with His perfect knowledge of everything there is to know, makes Him superior to every false god (vv. 21-29).

If you have trusted in Jesus Christ for your salvation, then He is your God. You are His people. He can be relied upon to work for your good, provide for your needs, equip you for any challenges you may face, and have complete knowledge of every situation that lies ahead of you. Will you choose afresh to trust His goodness today? If you have not trusted in God yet and become one of His children, please refer back to the Matters of the Heart section at the beginning of this book.

Journal

- Describe your relationship with God.

- Have you thought about the relationship between knowing God's character and your life change? Write down one thing you learned about this from this chapter.

- Think back to the three things you are most afraid of. How does the knowledge of God's presence in your life help you view these fears differently? Include Bible verses.

- Look at the larger context of today's verse. How do these realities apply to the things that bring you fear? Be specific.

Pray

Loving, Heavenly Father, thank You for promising to personally be with me in every trial I face. I choose to receive Your promised enablement, aid, and covenant love.

Thank You for using Your power for my benefit, and You protect me within the safety of Your hand.

Please teach me to trust Your goodness even when life is hard. I choose to believe what Your Word says and not what my circumstances or emotions may tell me that contradicts it. I will look expectantly for your help and provision in the difficulty I'm facing that has put me in fear: (name it).

I ask Your forgiveness for not trusting Your wisdom, care, power, and love. Please help me to choose to trust You each day, and please help me to glorify You as I do so. In Jesus' name, Amen.

Act

In order to firmly establish this idea in your mind and engrave it in your heart, it is necessary to contemplate on the verse that began this chapter. God is with you; He will hold and strengthen you. So don't fear. You can write that down and put it up on your refrigerator or write it in as a reminder with an alarm on your phone that will go off every morning. Do that right now and come back tomorrow.

DAY FIVE

Don't Worry About Anything

Read: Be anxious for nothing, but in everything by prayer and supplication, with thanksgiving, let your requests be made known to God; and the peace of God, which surpasses all understanding, will guard your hearts and minds through Christ Jesus. Philippians 4:6-7

Reflect

Could it really be possible to stop giving in to anxiety and worry? You just read my two favorite verses in the world. When I was in my darkest hours, those are the verses that made me realize a few important things.

1. I *can* stop being anxious.

According to these verses, God tells us not to be anxious. In fact, He commands. That must mean it's possible to live without anxiety. It would be unreasonable for Him to command us to do something that is not attainable. Furthermore, if God commands us not to do something and we do it, it could be considered a sin. God would not command us to do anything we cannot do.

2. When I'm anxious, I should pray.

Keep in mind there are two things to understand about this fight:

Experiencing the temptation to be anxious, and giving into the anxiety, are two different things.

Temptation and sin are not the same thing. The temptation to consume ice cream may arise, but you will not encounter the repercussions of consuming ice cream on a large scale until you have surrendered to the temptation and indulged in it. It's very important to recognize the difference. Situations that lead to anxiety will not magically disappear once you reach some level of spiritual maturity. You will always be tempted by anxiety!

You're likely to experience the onset of anxious thoughts time and time again throughout your entire life. Temptations to be worried or apprehensive can appear suddenly and without warning.

BUT God is the one who provides the ability and strength to grow in battling anxiety.

Surviving the assaults of anxiety is not meant to be a solo journey. Relying solely on yourself to overcome anxiety by working harder is likely to result in failure. You need to pray and ask God for help.

As a created being, you are prone to weakness, sin, and failure, like all mankind.

God is perfect, but we are not. Becoming dependent on Him to help you change is the only lasting solution. Prayer is the means of connecting to the power that God is willing to give you, which enables you to follow His commands.

Although we recognize that God is the one who brings growth, it does not eliminate our responsibility to grow. The expression "let go and let God" is not a very good strategy for overcoming anxiety.

You play a significant role in your own spiritual growth. Developing a habit of communicating with God about your anxiety and asking Him for help is essential. Prayer is talking to God; supplication is asking God.

If you're not already in the habit of praying, start small and ask Him for help. You can start by just saying, "Help!" This may seem weird, but even the desire to pray comes from Him. He is the one who draws you closer to Him. But we do have a part to play.

Draw near to God and He will draw near to you.
James 4:8

Remember, the moment you start to feel anxious, turn to God in prayer and draw closer to Him.

3. I thank God even when I don't feel it is working.

God is not a magical genie that is going to change your life in an instant. God is your parent who will guide you into spiritual growth. This journey of getting rid of anxiety is yours. He is there to help you through it so that you can become stronger. There is peace in knowing that God is on your side as you navigate through this anxiety ridden world. Thank Him! Thank Him for the journey until it's complete. Then thank Him again for taking you through it.

It's only then, that you can see some glimpse of...

"The peace of God, which surpasses all understanding, will guard your hearts and minds through Christ Jesus." Philippians 4:7

Journal

- How quickly do you recognize when a temptation to worry comes along?

- What circumstances cause you to fall into thinking, "If I just try harder, I can conquer this anxiety"?

- Do you consciously ask God for help when anxiety comes along, or are you more apt to figure it out yourself?

- Describe what your present prayer life looks like. What would you like to change about your habit of communing with God?

Pray

Heavenly Father, I want to grow in my communion with You. Help me to remember to thank You for all You have already done for me. I know that I need your help to overcome my fear and anxiety.

I recognize how easily I can depend on myself instead of casting my burdens on You. I recognize this can add to my anxiety, because I forget You in the midst of the trouble. Instead of immediately asking You for help, I try to handle everything on my own, which makes my anxiety even worse.

Please teach me to run to You quickly. Deepen my trust in You, because You want to hear from me. In Jesus' name, Amen.

Act

Think about something you use every day. Something that never leaves home without you, and you will always have with you. This can be your phone, wallet, purse, book, etc. Take a small sticky note or paper with tape and stick it to that thing. Simply write the word "HELP" on it. When you are tempted to feel anxious about anything, look at it and know you have help by just asking God. Even if it is just for a few seconds, pray. Make this a habit. Don't be ashamed to ask your Father for help in prayer and thank Him for being there.

DAY SIX

My Peace, I Give You

Read: *Peace I leave with you, My peace I give to you; not as the world gives do I give to you. Let not your heart be troubled, neither let it be afraid. John 14:27*

Reflect

Put yourself in the sandals of the Apostles. Jesus is hours away from His crucifixion, and He has told you—after three-plus years of constant companionship—that He is going back to the Father. Your Lord, friend, teacher, and protector will soon be gone. You must carry on His work, in a hostile world, on your own.

How would you have felt? Powerless. Fearful. Daunted. Who will take care of you? How will you accomplish the task He is leaving for you? What will your future be like?

The Lord did not leave them in the dark, and neither did He leave us.

John 14 is overflowing with promises of His help, plan, and presence. I recommend that you take the time to read the entire chapter for yourself. Jesus opens the chapter by assuring the men He is leaving them only to prepare a place for them in Heaven, to which He will one day come and take them (v.1-3)

The peace that Jesus promises us is not just an absence of conflict or trouble. It is a deep sense of calmness, assurance, and contentment that comes from the understanding that we are loved by God and that we are in His care. It is a peace that transcends all understanding, guarding our hearts and minds in Christ Jesus. He promises answered prayer (v.12-14), and He also repeatedly mentions the necessity of obedience (v.15, 21-24).

Why are we not alone even though Jesus left to be with the Father? Our verse falls in the context of Jesus' promise of the Holy Spirit. The verse just before says the Spirit will guide disciples into all truth (v. 26), while the next reaffirms Jesus' promise to be with His people by the Spirit (v. 28). Earlier, after mentioning the Holy Spirit, Jesus says He will not leave them as orphans; He will come to them (vv. 16-18).

We have peace only because Jesus has sworn to be with us, and in us, by His Holy Spirit.

The Lord is no longer physically present on earth; He is currently in Heaven and awaits His return. But His Spirit dwells within every believer, and that promise of His personal presence is the source of our hope.

This peace is not from the world.

The world looks to favorable circumstances to be sources of peace. Perhaps you feel all your anxiety and fear of the future will be solved with money. Or maybe it will all disappear when you find the perfect spouse. Will it finally be gone when you find the perfect God? These are good things and can be blessings from God. But they are not the source of peace, security, or hope. Only God Himself is peace. Because He is not dependent on the world, our hope in Him is unassailable.

This peace leads to freedom from fear.

We can only experience true freedom from fear that dominates our lives when we trust in God's promises to us through Christ and rest in them.

Our focus must be on Him, His character, and His promises, not on our circumstances. The things that you cannot control are perfectly manageable by God!

Journal

- In some ways, today's verse parallels or expands upon yesterday's verses. Reflect on both passages. What similarities do you see? How do they inform or complement one another?

- In what ways does having Jesus personally indwelling in you through His Spirit aid in conquering fear?

- Have you considered how the presence of Jesus within you relates to your ability to overcome fear? What new insights have you gained from today's devotional regarding this connection?

- What, if any, difference do you notice between the peace God gives and the peace that comes "from the world"? How might this difference impact your fearfulness?

Pray

Lord Jesus, thank You that You are personally present with me by Your Spirit. You have not left me alone but have chosen to dwell with and in me. Thank You that I can rely on Your powerful presence within me each day as I face the dark world around me.

Help me to appropriate the peace that is mine in Christ. You do not want me to be fearful, anguished, or overwhelmed by the things that terrify me. You have promised me peace because of what You did on the cross, and I choose to receive it with thanksgiving and joy.

Please fill me afresh with Your Holy Spirit. He is my peace, just as You are, and I surrender myself completely to His loving authority, influence, and care. Thank You that as He abides in and with me, I can know His blessing, power, and peace, and live in freedom from fear by faith.

Thank you for hearing my prayer that I have offered according to Your will, just as You promised (John 14:14). I offer You this day to accomplish Your perfect purposes in and through me, knowing that each step is overshadowed by Your covenant love.

In Jesus' name, Amen.

Act

Because of the relationship between peace and the Holy Spirit, you may want to personally invite Him (the Holy Spirit) to fill you. The Bible also calls the Holy Spirit our Comforter and Counselor. Remember, Jesus said He is here so that your heart will not be troubled and you will not be afraid. Ask God to speak specifically to the things that make you fearful and thank Him for His promise of peace.

DAY SEVEN

God's Perfect Love

Read: *"There is no fear in love; but perfect love casts out fear, because fear involves torment." 1 John 4:18*

Reflect

Because you are God's child, you can know that He loves you very much. He gave His only Son for you! Because of this, you have no need to fear. God has cast it all away! Torment comes when we don't fully rely on or trust in the love God has already shown us.

Regardless of the circumstances you find yourself in, you can run to God in prayer just as we run to our parents in times of need. Just like a parent would enjoy talking with a cherished child, our heavenly Father wants to hear all the care you want to discuss -the good, the bad, and the ugly. He knows it all, anyway.

Rejoice in the fact that, as a believer in Jesus Christ, you can speak directly with the Maker of the universe about EVERY detail of your life, whether large or small, without fear.

And everything really does mean everything! Prayer was not meant to only be used in crises. Avoid resigning yourself to tolerating things the way they are. Go to Him! Be brutally honest. Be humble. Admit your need for his help.

You don't need to be fancy when you talk to God. Prayer is simply talking with God, the way you'd talk with a close friend. Addressing worries in your life should begin with prayer. You can praise and worship Him as part of prayer, as well as share your worries and thoughts with Him.

You are welcome to ask God for help or a favor, remaining mindful of his power and might. We approach Him reverently, but at the same time, with freedom and confidence — not timidly — since Christ paved the way.

Prayer not only serves as a means of connecting with God, but it is also a time to receive instructions from Him. When you pray, it should never be all about you but about others as well. We will talk more about this tomorrow, but God wants you to pray for others before yourself. He wants you to have the heart of Jesus when you come to Him. When you pray and love others first, you can rest in the assurance that God loves you!

Journal

- How does it encourage you that you are God's child?

- Are there ever times when you don't pray because you think the request is too small? What seems too small to you?

- Do you feel like you need to pray in a "fancy" way when you talk to God? How do you talk to Him?

- What can you do to develop a sense of freedom to always come to God with all your requests?

- How has your relationship with God improved after spending the past week reading, reflecting, praying, journaling, and taking action?

Pray

Father, thank you for your perfect love that casts out all fear. If You gave Your only Son for me, what could I ever be afraid of? Please help me to rest in and trust your perfect love for me. When I'm anxious or worried, help me to find peace in your deep love.

Forgive me for the times when I haven't rested in your perfect love. For the times I have let my imagination get the best of me. For the times I have given in to sinful worry rather than trust my good and loving Father.

Right now, I give all my worries to you. I choose to let your amazing, powerful love drive out all the fears and anxieties that are plaguing me. I receive the peace you offer. In Jesus' name, amen.

Act

Think of three things you are anxious or worried about today. Write them down on a scale of 1 - 10 how anxious you are about each of them. Take the one with the highest number. Meditate on whether that anxiety is valid. Have you asked God for help? Take the time to think about all the ways God has already begun helping in that area. Once you have done that, can you rate that anxiety with a lower number? Do this for the other two as well.

DAY EIGHT

Being Perfected In Love

Read: *"There is no fear in love; but perfect love casts out fear, because fear involves torment. But he who fears has not been made perfect in love." 1 John 4:18*

Reflection

Today's verse falls in a section about God's love for us and ours for Him and each other (1 John 4:7-21). John is speaking about love's importance to the daily Christian life. In this verse's paragraph, John moves from abiding in Christ and God (vv. 13-15) to knowing and believing God's love (v. 16).

God's love is perfect toward us, but what does it mean to be made perfect in love? After all, this verse suggests that if we have fear, then we have not been made complete in love.

Love being "perfected" means that it has achieved its intended purpose or goal. John says it is by remaining in Christ and in love for Him and others that love is brought to completion in us (vv. 16-17). In other words, love has a goal. It has an intended effect. It has a purpose.

When you believed in the Lord Jesus Christ, God began a "sanctification" process in you. God is constantly working on us to make us more like Jesus. One of the great attributes of Jesus is that He was selfless. He thought of others before Himself. This is reflected in the way He allowed Himself to be crucified for us, even though we didn't deserve it.

Most of our fear, worry, and anxiety are internal. We are worried about *ourselves*; we are anxious about something that may or may not happen to *us*. It is all about *us*. We worry because we are only thinking of *ourselves*.

God calls us to take all the love He gave us and give it to someone else! If God has shown us love, then it is our duty to show love to others as well. God is sanctifying us and making us more and more like Jesus so that we can live a selfless life just like He did.

Becoming perfect in love requires effort on our part. Although God will lead us through His Holy Spirit, we must take the initiative to act. We must be willing to become perfect in love and translate that into a tangible action that benefits others.

The idea is simple. If you are busy thinking of others and taking the necessary steps to help someone else daily, you *will* worry less about yourself —Selflessness.

There was a time I remember getting paid on Friday, and by Saturday, my entire check was gone except for $20. I kept that $20 in my pocket for 3 days. I was always worried about losing it or spending it foolishly. Then I came across a friend who needed it more than I did. I realized that I had everything I needed for the rest of the week. God had already loved me enough to take care of me, so why was I holding onto this $20 with worry? I gave it to them and suddenly felt a weight lifted from my life. I felt joyful to give It out, and every concern about the money dissipated. This act of giving helped me grow in perfect love and eliminate any trace of fear.

If we are fearful, then something is lacking in our love.

Today's verse makes that clear:

"But he who fears has not been made perfect in love."

In this context, the fear is specifically fearing condemnation on the day of judgment, but in principle, it can apply to any fear.

Fear can be God's wake-up call for you to mature in your love for Him and others.

This is particularly true with respect to your confidence in Him and His goodness. If you are fearful, it implies that you are doubting God's goodness and ability to take care of you on some level. You don't trust Him, and so you are withholding a part of yourself from Him. This is a lack of love for God.

If we trust God, we will love Him. If we love Him, we will trust Him, trust His timing, perspective, plans, orchestration of life's events, and everything else He is and does.

As our love for Him matures and grows, we will trust Him more, which means we will be less fearful and more assured of His watchful care. This allows us to have the freedom to love others.

Journal

- How important do you think the love for God and others is to the daily Christian life? What, if anything, changed in you after reading this chapter?

- Today's devotional talked a lot about the importance of love being "perfected" or brought to its intended goal in our lives. Apart from its relationship to fear, what are some areas the Lord brought to mind about how you still need to grow in love?

- Now, let's consider the relationship between fear and love. Had you realized that being dominated by fear indicated a lack of love? Being as specific as possible, what do you think the relationship is between your specific fears and a possible lack of love?

- What is the relationship between love and faith? Be specific.

- If you have determined that your fears are in part related to a lack of love, ask the Lord to show you how increasing in love can help you overcome them. Write down any insights He gives you below.

- How does your love for God address what others might see as His lack of faithfulness, compassion, concern, or willingness to help you? How could these love-borne insights into His character help you give an answer for the hope that is in you (1 Peter 3:15) to people who might question His goodness?

Act

Choose to cultivate a love for God and others.

Lack of love is often revealed in life-dominating fear. Choose to receive this as God is prodding you to examine your heart for incompleteness in your love for Him and His people. Choose to receive and trust God's faithful love for you in Christ.

Now the hard part. Remember the three things you wrote down yesterday? You rated those on a scale of 1 – 10. Is there one that is still making you anxious? How can you overcome that anxiety by helping someone else?

For example, if you are anxious about what you will eat, who can you feed tomorrow? If you are concerned about money, have you considered identifying someone who may be in greater need of money than you and giving it to them? This practice is imperative to finding freedom in your life. Plan to do this tomorrow. Commit to it and pray to God for the strength to get it done.

DAY NINE

Trusting His Faithfulness

Read: *"Therefore know that the Lord your God, He is God, the faithful God who keeps covenant and mercy for a thousand generations with those who love Him and keep His commandments" Deuteronomy 7:9*

Reflect

Trusting in God's faithfulness means that you believe that He is who He says He is and He will do what He has promised. It means that you can look back at His track record of faithfulness in your own life, as well as in the lives of others throughout history, and know that He will continue to be faithful to you in the present and in the future.

The best weapon you have against fear is a vibrant relationship with God. As you know Him more intimately, you become more confident in His character and ability to protect you.

But this increased confidence requires accurate knowledge of His attributes and ways—you must know Him as He is, as He has revealed Himself to be.

Today's passage falls in the context of reassuring God's people of His ability to move heaven and earth to keep His promises. They are about to enter the promised land, and they will have an uphill battle in claiming what God has provided for them. God assures them of His future protection of them based on His past provision.

God encourages them to look back to their rescue from Egypt as the foundation for their present confidence in Him. The "therefore" refers to verse 8's rehearsal of God's love for them and His acting powerfully to rescue them from enslavement under Pharaoh.

God is a covenant-keeping, faithful God. He's proven it to them. Their future is secure because God will be the same as He has been in the past.

Later in the chapter, God explicitly brings up what they are to do if they are afraid of the wicked people who presently occupy the land:

> *"you shall not be afraid of them, but you shall remember well what the Lord your God did to Pharaoh and to all Egypt:" (v. 18).*

Just as God was unswervingly faithful to Israel, He is faithful to you. Like the Israelites, you are a member of God's people. He makes a covenant with you and can be trusted to keep it. When you are afraid, He tells you to remember how He has already been faithful to you throughout your life in order to know He will continue to be today.

Reminding yourself of God's character is essential to freedom from fear.

You must rest in who He is. His faithfulness means He can be trusted to keep His promises, to care for you, to uphold you, and to meet your needs. If He were a liar, His promises would mean nothing. But because He is utterly trustworthy, His promises can be fully relied upon.

So, trust in His faithfulness today, and cast all your fears and anxieties on Him. Remember that He is the faithful God who loves you and is always with you, no matter what you may face. When you trust in His faithfulness, you can live with peace, joy, and hope, knowing that He is working all things together for your good.

Journal

- How has this chapter clarified your view of God?

- Name three times when you have seen God's deliverance and faithfulness in your past. How does this speak to the things which presently make you fearful?

- Using the verse and its context mentioned in this chapter, write out how God's faithfulness to you can help you overcome the things that make you afraid. Make the connections as direct as you can.

Pray

Dear Heavenly Father, I praise You for Your faithfulness to me. You will not leave or abandon me but have promised to do everything necessary to meet my needs and keep me safe.

When I look back over my life, I can see the instances of Your past faithfulness and provision (name them). This assurance comforts me, knowing that You will be just as faithful to me in the future as You were to Israel in the past. I can face the unknown, knowing that You will come through for me.

Thank You for being completely trustworthy in doing what You have promised. While I do not know what tomorrow holds, You are already aware of it and will give me whatever I genuinely need right on time and not before.

Please help me to have greater confidence in Your faithful care, provision, love, protection, and kindness.

I choose to trust who You are and not let my circumstances dictate my view of You.

Please manifest Your faithfulness to me in the areas that most cause me to fear (name them). Thank You. In Jesus' name, Amen.

Act

Choose a verse on God's faithfulness (either this one or another that is meaningful to you) and memorize it. You can use your Bible or websites like biblegateway.com to search by topic. Choose the one that really speaks to you. Write the verse and its reference below to help you remember it. Speak it over and over again until you memorize it.

Could Anxiety Be A Blessing?

Read: *"In the multitude of my anxieties within me, Your comforts delight my soul." Psalm 94:19*

Reflect

Anxiety never feels like it's a good thing.

Worries can make life seem out of control, overwhelming, and difficult, leading you to believe that nothing will ever change and that it's too much to cope with. You can end up living in "survival mode" as anxious thoughts swirl around you unchecked.

But here's a unique viewpoint to consider:

It Is possible that battling anxious thoughts could benefit you in ways you are not seeing clearly right now.

- What if anxiety guides you into a greater awareness of God's great power and love or helps you to see the truth more clearly?

- What if the outcome is a more peaceful, patient, and mature version of yourself, an individual who loves, trusts, and cherishes God more as a result?

As you experience anxious thoughts and feelings, consider the different things that God might be teaching you. Maybe you're learning that you don't have control over others or situations that tempt you to be worried. Or that you're not as powerful or wise as God, who is able to bring change.

Anxiety can also be a reminder of your dependence on God. When you feel anxious, you may be more likely to turn to Him in prayer and seek His guidance. This can help you to deepen your relationship with God and trust in His plan for your life.

In addition, anxiety may be a catalyst for personal growth and development. When you experience anxiety, it may be an indication that you need to make changes or take action to address a particular issue in your life. This can motivate you to step outside of your comfort zone and take risks that lead to personal growth and development.

Ultimately, Psalm 94:19 should remind you that even amid anxiety, God's consolation can bring you joy. By turning to Him in your struggle, you can find comfort and reassurance that He is with you always. And when you view anxiety as an opportunity for personal growth and development, you can find meaning and purpose in your struggles.

Yes, anxiety can be challenging, but it can also be a blessing in disguise. By turning to God for comfort and guidance, we can find joy in our struggles. And by viewing anxiety as an opportunity for personal growth, we can find meaning and purpose in our struggles.

Let anxiety be a teacher for you. Let it push you towards God, so you can learn the good things that He wants to teach you.

Journal

- Name something that would make your struggles with anxiety worth going through.

- What are some of the lies you are tempted to believe when anxiety arrives unexpectedly?

- How might you change your perspective on anxiety to view yourself as a soldier who is equipped for battle?

Pray

Father, I thank you that you are with me even when I'm experiencing anxiety. Help me to understand that You are teaching me good, valuable things even during tough times. You're never absent from my life. You're always at work in me, even when I'm anxious. In Jesus' name, amen.

Act

It's time to rest. It's time to reflect on the past week. It's time to recommit. If you feel like quitting, pull out that envelope and remember what you wrote. Pray and ask God for help to finish this program. You can do it! He is with you!

DAY ELEVEN

Gratefulness Drives Out Worry

Read: *"If you then, being evil, know how to give good gifts to your children, how much more will your Father who is in heaven give good things to those who ask Him!" Matthew 7:11*

Reflect

Life can get overwhelming. We may be easily discouraged or burned out when things are beyond our control. How do we turn our gaze away from the challenges and turn to God?

One of the best ways is to reflect on past and current blessings.

You can offer thanks to God for all He has given you and all He has done on your behalf.

There is so much you can thank Him for — from the small, daily provisions to the visibly significant ones.

- Waking up to a new day
- A kindness or financial provision that was unexpected
- Beautiful weather
- Healing from illness
- Utilities and transportation
- Time with friends and family
- An enjoyable meal

The list of things to be thankful for is endless!

An attitude of thanksgiving has a connection to experiencing inward peace.

Reflecting on God's goodness reminds you that He is good and sovereign. It's not up to you, other people, or your circumstances to determine what will happen. When you're feeling anxious or worried, try flipping the script. Instead of focusing on the negative things in front of you, turn your attention to all the amazing ways that God has blessed you!

Moreover, reflecting on God's goodness helps you to cultivate a spirit of gratefulness in your heart. When you focus on all the blessings He has given you, you can't help but feel grateful for His goodness and grace. This gratefulness can help to shift your focus away from your worries and onto the blessings in your life.

Journal

- How does gratefulness help you to overcome worry?

- How can you remind yourself to focus on your blessings rather than negative things?

- What steps can you take to incorporate more gratefulness into your life?

Pray

Father, thank you for all the amazing blessings you have poured into my life. They are beyond counting! The greatest blessing that I have is my relationship with you. The fact that I can call you Father is simply incredible.

But beyond that, you have given me so much more.

Please forgive me for the times when I have focused more on what I lack than on what I possess. Forgive me for being ungrateful despite having received so very much.

Today, I am choosing gratefulness over anxiety. In Jesus' name, amen.

Act

Pull out a journal and start writing down all the blessings you have experienced in life. Write down everything for which you are thankful and grateful. With each blessing or thanksgiving, pause and thank God for it. Try to make this a daily habit if possible. Set a thanksgiving alarm on your phone or post a question on your refrigerator, "What three things are you thankful for today?" Try to make the answers different every day. The more grateful you are, the less anxious you will be.

DAY TWELVE

Fighting Fear When You've Made A Mess

Read: *"Whenever I am afraid, I will trust in You. In God (I will praise His word), In God I have put my trust; I will not fear. What can flesh do to me?" Psalm 56:3-4*

Reflect

David was in trouble. He was taken captive by the Philistines in their city of Gath, and only by pretending to be a madman was he able to escape and return home (see 1 Samuel 21:10-15). Psalm 56 records how he chose to trust God rather than give in to his very real fears during that deadly circumstance.

Moreover, he was in trouble because of his own poor decisions.

David was in Gath because he was fleeing from people who wanted him dead. It wasn't the fleeing that was the problem but fleeing to a Gentile land outside the protection and blessing of God.

David's response to the sinful behavior of others compounded his fearful situation.

Yet David still asks God to rescue him from the consequences of his poor choices. That should be deeply encouraging to us!

God does not shame us for petitioning Him for deliverance if our stupidity has gotten us into hot water. He is merciful and gracious, and if we choose to trust Him now, He can bring good out of our past bad decisions.

David responds in faith despite his foolishness and his enemies' threats. He was afraid of Saul and his men. He was afraid of the Philistines. He was probably ashamed of having to look like an insane fool before his enemies. But he chose to respond based on God's character, not on his emotions or circumstances.

Perhaps David composed this psalm as he returned to Israel. It is possible that he was contemplating the recent events, seeking the Lord for guidance and comfort, and as he did, the words to this psalm gradually took shape in his thoughts.

He knew the goodness and faithfulness of God. He chose faith over fear. He chose confidence in God's promises.

If you are afraid because of the effects of your foolish or sinful choices, take heart. God has not forsaken you. God can be trusted to bring good out of difficulty, even when it's caused in large part or small by your unbelief, foolishness, fear, or pride.

Choose to trust God's character and promises, especially when you have made your own mess.

As you trust in God's faithfulness and power, you can have hope for the future. You can believe that God would bring good out of your mess and that He can use your mistakes to teach you important lessons and shape you into the person He wants you to be.

You can acknowledge your mistakes, take responsibility for them, and trust in God's power and love to guide you through the challenges you face. As you focus on His promises and trust in His faithfulness, you can have hope for the future and the courage to make things right. So, turn to God today and trust in His unfailing love and grace.

Journal

- Have your sinful or unwise choices contributed to your experience of fear? Briefly write them down below.

- If these choices have contributed to your fear, do you secretly believe you deserve it or that God is punishing you?

- How does David's experience help you combat this false view of God?

- Do you believe God can set you free from fear, from your sinful or foolish choices, and from their consequences, even though your circumstances may contradict that?

- Write down one thing you learned about God from this chapter and how it can help you overcome fear.

____

____

____

Pray

Gracious, Heavenly Father, thank You that because of Christ, You are there for me even when I have failed You. Thank You that my unbelief does not have to render me useless or forsaken to You. Thank You that You can use my poor choices for Your purposes and to teach me to trust You better.

I humbly seek Your forgiveness for the decisions I have made that have played a role in causing the current state of fear that I find myself in (name them).

Thank You that You can bring good out of these sinful choices and that I have an opportunity to choose to trust You again. Thank You for remaining faithful to me and drawing me back to You even when I have failed.

Please remind me of Your forgiveness and faithfulness. Please do not let the awareness of my sin or stupidity drown out confidence in Your willingness to rescue, bless, encourage, strengthen, restore, heal, and vindicate me. Instead, I choose to believe You based on Your Word, not my feelings or circumstances.

Thank You for hearing my prayer. I thank You for how You will use these experiences to enlarge my faith in You and Your willingness to bless me as I choose to trust You.

In Jesus' name, Amen.

Act

There is a scene in the movie *O Brother, Where Are Thou?* where one of the three leads in the film gives their life to Christ and gets baptized in the Mississippi River. The three characters (Pete, Delmar, and Everett, played by George Clooney) have escaped from prison and are on the run. Delmar emerges with the excitement that he has been forgiven by the Lord for all his wrong-doings, so Pete follows.

While this is true, the State of Mississippi is still after them. This confuses Pete, who then says, "The preacher said it absolved us."

"For him, not for the law!" exclaims Everett.

Delmar interrupts, "But there were witnesses who saw us redeemed!"

Finally, George Clooney gives a funny delivery to the next line as Everett, "That's not the issue, Delmar. Even if it did put you square with the Lord, the State of Mississippi is more hard-nosed."

The thought of this next action step may make you feel anxious, but doing this will forever rid you of this particular anxiety.

It is time to right the wrong.

Think of one sin or mistake you have made in the past that is correctable. It could have been something you did to yourself or someone else. It needs to be something you can change or make up to someone. It doesn't have to be huge or drastic. Start with something small. Take the time to brainstorm how you can fix this mistake.

Remember, God is with you. Ask Him for help. Once you have done this, you will feel the release of all that built-up anxiety over this particular mistake just disappear. Take the time to do it this week. It will change your life.

Fighting Fear When You Didn't Make The Mess

Read: *"Now when He got into a boat, His disciples followed Him. And suddenly a great tempest arose on the sea, so that the boat was covered with the waves. But He was asleep. Then His disciples came to Him and awoke Him, saying, "Lord, save us! We are perishing!""* Matthew 8:23-25

Reflect

I wonder how many of us would have reacted just like the disciples did. Unlike our last chapter, this is an example of a situation we didn't put ourselves in. I, myself, would have cried out for help as well. Jesus was asleep in the boat the entire time they thought they were going to die. Did Jesus know the storm was coming? Did He know this was going to happen? Of course, He did; He initiated crossing over the lake. He was teaching them how to trust Him. They needed to learn to believe in Him, and have faith in Him, even though it seemed their lives were in danger.

There are things that happen in our lives that are truly scary. They bring us fear and anxiety. Some circumstances might even threaten our lives. But it is important to remember that Jesus is there.

Meditate on this thought. What if they had not cried out to Jesus to wake Him? I believe Jesus intended to sleep through the storm. The storm seemed dangerous, but Jesus knew it wouldn't kill them. What if they had taken a different approach? What if they had decided to learn from the storm?

The disciples could have trusted in the fact that Jesus was with them and would have never steered them wrong. They allowed their lack of faith to overwhelm them, and the waves were a perfect metaphor for that. They didn't believe Jesus wouldn't perish in the storm because they didn't fully understand who He was yet. So they shook Him awake.

"But He said to them, "Why are you fearful, O you of little faith?" Then He arose and rebuked the winds and the sea, and there was a great calm. So the men marveled, saying, "Who can this be, that even the winds and the sea obey Him?" Matthew 8:26-27

Knowing that Jesus was the Son of God and that even the winds and the sea obey Him is something you and I should also consider. It doesn't matter how big our waves are in life; Jesus is in full control on our behalf.

The storm would have lasted longer if they had allowed Jesus to sleep. They would have gone through it until they reached their destination. He was going to let them go through the storm because He was there the whole time. Why? To learn to rely on Him and have faith in Him. If they had that faith, they would have remained calm in the storm.

Journal

- Do you recall an experience when you felt you were in the storm?

- What was your first instinct when this happened?

- How would that situation have played out differently if you had trusted that Jesus was with you through it all?

- What will you do next time?

Pray

Lord, thank You because no matter what storms I'm in or have experienced, You have been with me. Not only that, You are in control because the winds and the waves obey You! I know that even though the storms can be overwhelming and more than I can bare, You can hear my cries and help me through. I know I can cry out to You, and You will be there. Help me to grow more in faith so that I can endure more and more for Your glory! In Jesus' name, Amen.

Act

Let's practice this. Think of a time in your past when the situation you were in was immensely overwhelming. You know the kind. A time you felt you would never get out of that situation. A time when it was hard to imagine that Jesus was with you the whole time.

But here you are. You did get out of it. Perhaps you even learned from it. Now, write for 5 minutes without stopping. Write down what that situation was, how you felt when you were in it, what you learned, and then finally, looking back, would you change the experience today?

Some of you may be going through something right now. Something so overwhelming you can't see a way out. The waves are too big. To you, I say, write for 5 minutes. Write down the situation you are in and how you feel about it. Then, write down 3 things you could potentially learn from what you are going through. Will this bring you closer to God? To a loved one? Would you change it all? You never know if God is using this situation to help you become stronger for the next waves that may be coming.

He Is With You In The Valley

Read: *"Yea, though I walk through the valley of the shadow of death, I will fear no evil; For You are with me; Your rod and Your staff, they comfort me." Psalm 23:4*

Reflect

Psalm 23 is a beautiful Psalm. We are going to read verses 1 – 3 in order to get the meaning of verse 4.

The Lord is my shepherd;
I shall not want.
He makes me to lie down in green pastures;
He leads me beside the still waters.
He restores my soul;
He leads me in the paths of righteousness
For His name's sake.

Take notice of what's happening here. The Lord is your shepherd. Because He is your Shepherd, you will never be in need (I shall not want). Because He is your shepherd, he makes you… He leads you… He restores you…

Now, if the Shepherd is making, leading, and restoring you the entire journey, then how did you get yourself into the valley of death? Here's a controversial thought. You are in the valley of the shadow of death because He took you there.

That is the only explanation. You will not fear any evil because just as He was there with you through the green pastures and still waters, He is also there with you in the valley.

What makes a valley?

When we picture a valley, it is often depicted as being surrounded by two mountains, with one situated on each side. You leave the comfort of the green hills and descend into the shadows the mountains have created in that valley. It is very gloomy. Animals hide in the rocks below, waiting for prey. Danger lurks around every corner. You navigate through a valley by progressing towards the end, where a glimmer of light is visible, which typically represents safety and the way out.

When we think of valleys in our lives, we think of trouble. Very often in life, we are on green pastures and drinking of the still beautiful waters, and at other times we are in the midst of despair, in darkness, wondering if there is light on the other side. While we walk through our "valleys" in life, we feel our way through it all and learn things. We realize things we didn't know before, like, perhaps, how great the green pastures actually were. We begin to change on the inside. We realize we need to rely on Him. Let's read our verse one more time.

Yea, though I walk through the valley of the shadow of death, I will fear no evil; For You are with me; Your rod and Your staff, they comfort me."
Psalm 23:4

Suddenly it hits us. His rod and staff, His discipline, although painful at times, has never let us down. They have guided us in the right direction; they have never failed us. His rod and staff have made us lie down in green pastures when we didn't realize we were tired. They led us to water when we were thirsty. They restored our souls when we were down. More importantly, they led us in the paths of righteousness. They help us grow in the trials of life. The fact that Jesus has been in control allows us to feel and say, "Your rod and Your staff, they comfort me!

In the valley, God refines us, helping us through our darkest times, through our challenges, anxieties, mistakes, and fears. Let's trust His rod and staff to comfort us in our time of need.

Journal

- How have you fought against his rod and staff as He tried to guide you into righteousness?

- Can you think of a time you felt Him prodding at you before you made your way down into the valley?

- When you were in the valley, did you feel as though Jesus was not there with you even though He was? What will you do the next time to remind yourself that He is with you and will guide you out?

- How will you allow His discipline to comfort you?

- How has your relationship with God improved after spending the past week reading, reflecting, praying, journaling, and taking action?

Pray

Lord, forgive me for not realizing that it is You who guides me, comforts me, restores me, and makes me get some rest when I need it most. Help me to rely on your rod and staff as guidance and comfort. Show me that learning to be in Your righteousness may keep me away from the darkness. Keep me by Your side as my Shepherd. In Jesus Name, Amen.

Act

Grab a piece of string and wrap it around your finger or a bracelet. It's the oldest trick in the book to remind yourself of something. In this case, you will constantly remind yourself of God's presence in your life. Whenever you are going to make a decision, look at that string. Whenever you are feeling alone, look at the string. Whenever you are thirsty, look at that string and remember that He guides you, leads you, makes you, and comforts you always. All you have to do is remember, close your eyes, and thank Him.

DAY FIFTEEN

He Cares For You

Read: *"casting all your care upon Him, for He cares for you."*
1 Peter 5:7

Reflect

One of the greatest anxieties I have been working on is complete faith in God when it comes to my family. When I think of death, I am not so much worried about death but about who I'm leaving behind. I worry about how my children will cope when I'm gone. At present, I am the center of my two-year-old's world. What would happen to her if her entire world was suddenly taken away from her? What about finances? Have I done what I need to do to leave them what they need?

As humans, we tend to carry our burdens and worries with us wherever we go. We often feel overwhelmed and stressed by our problems, fears, and uncertainties. However, the Bible teaches us to cast our cares upon God, and He promises to take care of us when we do.

This verse reminds us that we aren't meant to carry our burdens on our own. Instead, God wants to bear those burdens with us. He wants to relieve us of our worries and anxieties so that we can experience peace and joy.

When we cast our cares upon God, it requires trust and faith in Him. We must believe that God is sovereign over all things and that He has the power to handle our problems in a way that is best for us. Sometimes, casting our cares upon God means letting go of our desire to control the situation and instead allowing God to work in His way and His timing.

Another crucial aspect of casting our cares upon God is prayer. As mentioned before, prayer is our way of communicating with God, and it allows us to express our fears, concerns, and worries to Him. Through prayer, we can ask God to guide us, provide for us, and give us peace in the midst of our troubles.

Casting our cares upon God also means seeking His will and direction for our lives. We must be willing to obey God's Word and follow His prompting in our lives. When we are aligned with God's will, we can trust that He will lead us in the right direction, even if it's not the direction we initially desired.

If I were to die tomorrow, I need to trust in Him that the timing was right and that He will watch over my family. The way I can grow my trust in Him is through prayer, reading the Bible, and obeying it. Learning what God wants me to do in this world so I am always in His will.

Casting our cares upon God requires trust, faith, prayer, and obedience. It's not always easy, but it's essential for our well-being and spiritual growth. When we give our burdens to God, we can experience joy, hope, and most importantly, peace in the midst of life's trials. So let us come to God with open hearts and minds, casting our cares upon Him, knowing that He cares for us.

Journal

- What are some of the worries and fears that you are currently carrying with you? How do these anxieties affect your mental, physical, and spiritual well-being?

- Why do you find it difficult to relinquish control and trust God with your problems?

- Do you currently have any unconfessed sins or areas of rebellion that may hinder your ability to fully trust God?

- Describe a time when you felt a sense of peace or comfort after praying about a specific worry or concern.

- Reflect on a time when you were able to cast your cares upon God and experience His provision and faithfulness. How can you use this as a source of encouragement and hope during times of future uncertainty or anxiety?

Pray

Lord, I have been trusting in my own strength, will, and wisdom when I should have been trusting in You, and I have seen that it is hard! If I'm lacking in faith, give me faith. If I need to pray more, remind me throughout the day. If I have been disobedient, correct me like a parent so I will have a better life. Relinquishing my anxiety and fear regarding the burdens that weigh heavily on me begins with entrusting them all to You! In Jesus, Name. Amen!

Act

Look at your journal answers. Write down some practical ways you can cultivate more trust and surrender in your relationship with Him. Think about areas in your life where you've been disobedient. Take some time to reflect and ask God to reveal any areas that need to be addressed. Now it's time to correct them. Confess them to God and decide on one action you will take today to bring you into obedience, surrender, and trust God for the result.

DAY SIXTEEN

Specific Prayers For Specific Worries

Read: *"Ask, and it will be given to you; seek, and you will find; knock, and it will be opened to you." Matthew 7:7*

Reflect

Throughout the Bible, God invites you to bring very specific prayer requests to Him. Of course, God already knows what you want or need because He sees and knows all. But you are told to ask for it.

If God already knows what we need, why should we ask Him? Because when we see God answer our specific prayers, it reminds us that He loves us and is active in our lives.

There is a handy acronym that can remind you to be specific in your requests. It spells out the word "GASP":

- God
- Answers
- Specific
- Prayers

Now gasp. Go ahead, inhale quickly as though something just frightened you. Every time something surprises you enough to *GASP*, it should be a reminder to you to pray. If you have a specific desire or requirement, it is important to communicate it to God in prayer, asking Him to provide it for you. Being specific in your prayers can help you focus your thoughts and intentions and allow you to better recognize when your prayers have been answered. Even though God knows what you want or need, He tells you to ask Him for it. It is for your benefit.

Of course, God can answer vague prayers, but being precise helps you recognize that you're actually taking part in what God is doing.

Specific answers to prayer are exciting! Sometimes it's easy to pray and forget. This makes it extremely difficult to realize when God has answered such prayers. Be specific and recognize it when it comes.

This is not to say that you will always obtain what you want or that God will always solve your problems the way you want. This does not promise that He will give you what you want at the time you desire, but He always hears you and works out what's best for you.

Sometimes things come out differently or at a different time. He is the Master Planner. I found the love of my life at 35 years old. I remember pleading with God, saying that I would never get married after 30 because it would be too late! I had to believe in God's timing.

Repeat after me, "I believe in God's timing." Speak it out loud until you believe it. "I believe in God's timing!"

Trying to control events according to my own timing reflects my impatience as an imperfect being. It shows greater trust in God's ability when I calm my soul and trust in Him even through uncertainty.

Journal

- Why is it important to pray even though God already knows what you need?

- Do you tend to pray specific or vague prayers? How can you make your prayers more specific?

- What specific things do you need to pray about today?

- Why is it good that God doesn't answer all our prayers in the ways or time frame we prefer?

Pray

Father, thank You for inviting me to bring my specific requests to You. I'm so grateful that I can come to You with all my needs, big and small. Forgive me for the times I have held back in prayer, not believing that You are eager to answer them.

Help me to trust you in times of waiting. I know that You love me and that everything You do for me is good. Even when I don't see the answer to prayer that I'm expecting, I know that you're working. In Jesus' name, Amen.

Act

It's time to be specific. Ask God for something specific. Be precise. Make sure it means something to you. Write it down and put it on your bathroom mirror. Look at it every day. Look for the answer every day. The more specific you are, the more it will mean something to you when you see the answer come!

Receiving God's Work In You

Read: *"For God has not given us a spirit of fear, but of power and of love and of a sound mind." 2 Timothy 1:7*

Reflect

Paul's protégé Timothy could be easily intimidated. Both in this letter and in allusions Paul makes elsewhere, it appears Timothy struggled with fear, particularly fear of what others thought of him, perhaps primarily because of his close association with the polarizing Apostle Paul.

Timothy is in Ephesus to continue Paul's work, and he faces an uphill battle. Paul's two letters to him explain this in detail, and even a casual reading can leave one feeling overwhelmed at everything Timothy was expected to impart and the hostile, immature context in which he ministered.

So, Paul begins by reminding Timothy of how God has equipped him. He says that God has given all Christians a spirit or disposition—not of fear, but of power, love, and a sound mind. When Timothy gives in to fear, he acts contrary to what is most deeply true about him as a Christian.

Rather than give in to timidity, we are to cultivate a strong spirit overflowing with these attributes.

God's grace at work in us means we can grow in spiritual power (enabled by the Holy Spirit to do the will of God), love (real affection and service for God and people), and discipline (a sound, self-controlled mind that gives rise to service that pleases God).

Each of these attributes contrasts with fear.

The first step to this is acknowledging and receiving God's promised work in you. If you are a Christian, God has given you this spirit. It isn't a question or up for debate. It's settled. But you can only operate in its provisions if you receive it as reality and acknowledge that it is God's work in you, not yours. Choose to trust what God says about you.

He has placed within you a new disposition towards Him, one that can channel His power, loves Him and others, and think in a clear, self-controlled way about reality.

There is nothing to be afraid of when God has done this work in you. Thank Him for it and be blessed as you rely on His transformation!

Journal

- Have you ever felt fearful of what other people think of you? Why, and what made you feel that way?

- Before reading this chapter, had you ever pondered the relationship between fear and how God has equipped you as a Christian? If so, how does what you thought back then compare to what you think now?

- What is most encouraging to you about the fact that God has placed this disposition in you of His own doing and not yours?

Prayer

Dear Heavenly Father, thank You for Your gracious work in me to combat fear. I am so encouraged to know that You have given me all I need to trust You and not be afraid—down to the very disposition You have given me as a Christian.

I realize now that when I give in to fear, I am acting contrary to everything I am as a Christian. Please forgive me for not appropriating what You have given me and done for me.

Please help me rest more in Your work in me rather than relying on my meager resources or abilities to face difficult circumstances.

Today, by faith, I welcome Your work in me. I choose to receive and believe what You have said about me and will rely on that rather than give in to fear and intimidation. I am grateful that You have embraced me under Your protection and guidance, providing me with all that is necessary to have faith in and follow You. In Jesus' name, Amen.

Act

Even while God is the one who put the disposition there, it is our responsibility to cultivate and live into it. Will you choose to do so? Look at each of the aspects of the disposition God has given you.

God's grace at work in us means we can grow in spiritual power (enabled by the Holy Spirit to do the will of God), love (real affection and service for God and people), and discipline (a sound, self-controlled mind that gives rise to service that pleases God).

Think of one way you can grow in spiritual power. How will you do the will of God today? How will you be of service to people today? How will you live in discipline today so that you can please God? Today your challenge is to do those three things. It doesn't have to be something big. It can be something small. Just take action!

DAY EIGHTEEN

All Things For Good

Read: *"And we know that all things work together for good to those who love God, to those who are the called according to His purpose." Romans 8:28*

Reflect

God is infinitely wise. The Bible reminds us that there are things that we, having finite minds and bodies, won't be able to comprehend here and now. There are things that we can't understand, no matter how much we try.

But because God is all-wise, good, and powerful, you can trust Him even when you don't understand your circumstances.

His plan for your life cannot be compared to what you might choose for yourself. You may not understand the challenges He allows to come into your life, but you can trust that his sovereignty is working all things together in the best possible way. Why? Because you are called according to His purpose!

This is the God that we serve. We wouldn't ask for anything less. We need help from someone wiser, stronger, and bigger. Someone who is awe-inspiring, whose sovereignty extends to all that's happening in your life, and who reigns over the universe.

Sovereignty means supreme power or authority. That's a great description of the realm of the Creator.

Even though you don't understand everything about Him, you can grow in your ability to trust Him.

Hold onto his promises and trust in his unfailing love and faithfulness. Even when you cannot see the good that God is working, you can have confidence that He is at work behind the scenes, using every circumstance to shape and mold you into the person He wants you to be.

Because God is loving, merciful, and kind in addition to all-knowing, you can trust that He knows exactly what types of needs or worries you are experiencing, and He is working it all together for good for you.

Journal

- How does it encourage you that God is all-wise?

- Is it hard for you to trust God's plan for your life? Why? How does Romans 8:28 help you trust God?

- What does it mean that God is sovereign over all things?

- When you reflect on the past, where have you clearly seen God intervening in your life?

Pray

Father, I thank you for working everything together for my good. There are a lot of things that I just don't understand. I don't know why You allow me to go through certain circumstances, but I trust that they have something to do with being called according to Your purpose.

I do believe that you know exactly what you're doing. Nothing is outside of your control. Nothing is beyond your knowledge and power. You absolutely know what is best for me and are causing all my circumstances to work together for good.

Though I may not know why something happens, I know that You're good, and nothing happens without your knowledge. Help me to rest in these truths when I feel anxious or worried. Help me to rest in you and find peace in you. In Jesus' name, amen.

Act

Take a sheet of paper and write down one circumstance in your life from the past in the center of the page. A situation or experience that may have been difficult to comprehend initially but with time has provided some clarity or insight. At the top of the page, write down the words "<u>For Good</u>" Write a list of good that has happened from that one circumstance. Think hard and find as many as you can. Put this on your wall in case you come across something you don't understand in the future.

DAY NINETEEN

God Is Dependable

Read: *"Fear not, for I am with you; Be not dismayed, for I am your God. I will strengthen you, Yes, I will help you, I will uphold you with My righteous right hand." Isaiah 41:10*

Reflect

From before the beginning of time and forever into eternity, our God has not, does not, and will not change. His character remains the same. His promises do not change.

As a believer, this is truly great news. God is reliable, and you can have unwavering trust and confidence in Him.

God is dependable. He is the rock on which you can build your life, the anchor that holds you steady through the storms of life. He is the same yesterday, today, and forever, and His love and faithfulness never fail.

Throughout the Scripture, we see countless examples of God's dependability. He is always faithful to His promises, always true to His character, and always present with His people.

One of the most powerful examples of God's dependability is found in Isaiah 40:28-31, which says:

"Have you not known? Have you not heard? The everlasting God, the Lord, The Creator of the ends of the earth, Neither faints nor is weary. His understanding is unsearchable. He gives power to the weak, And to those who have no might He increases strength. Even the youths shall faint and be weary, And the young men shall utterly fall, But those who

> *wait on the Lord Shall renew their strength; They shall mount up with wings like eagles, They shall run and not be weary, They shall walk and not faint."*

This passage should remind you that God is always dependable, even when you are not. He never grows tired or weary, and He is always there to give you strength when you are weak. As you put your hope and trust in Him, He renews your strength and enables you to overcome the challenges you face.

In a world that is constantly changing, where circumstances can shift in an instant, it can be easy to feel like everything is uncertain and unstable. But you can take comfort in the fact that God is always dependable. His love and faithfulness never fail, and His promises are sure.

You can trust God to write your life story.

When you take the time to look back, you will see evidence of his hand on your life. Reflecting on the past helps you realize that you can truly trust Him, even when anxious thoughts about a current situation assail you.

It's very possible that, in the years ahead, you will look back and ask yourself why you worried so much.

You will see all the ways that God guided you and led you. You will see how He protected you and even the ways that He redeemed the mistakes you made.

Anxiety often results from looking into the future and trying to figure out what will happen. You experience peace, on the other hand, when you trust the One who knows what the future holds and knows how He will lead you.

Ultimately, you must learn to trust in God's wisdom more than your own.

God's wisdom is more than just intelligence or knowing facts and figures. He understands everything, so His decisions are always the very best decisions. His competence and abilities are beyond your comprehension.

You can rest in those truths and find peace in your anxious heart.

Journal

- What are some ways in which you've seen God writing your life story?

- Do you struggle to believe that God is dependable? Why or why not?

- When are you most tempted to worry about the future?

- What does it look like when you trust God's wisdom rather than your own?

Pray

Father, I praise You that You are always dependable. You never change. All Your promises are trustworthy and will come to pass. While there is so much in life that is unreliable, You are a rock that I can always trust.

Forgive me for trying to figure out the future instead of remembering how You have taken care of me in the past. You know exactly where I'm headed, and You have good plans in store for me. Even when the future appears uncertain or unclear to me, I take comfort in knowing that it is always crystal clear to You, God. In Jesus' Name, Amen.

Act

The reason that God is so dependable is because He knows the end from the beginning. He has a plan that He has already seen play out. What is making you anxious or fearful right now? Is it something that hasn't happened yet? Does it live in a future you can't see? What is it? Once you have it clear in your mind, what kind of planning can you do to make you less anxious or fearful about it? If you are afraid of something as small as running out of gas, can you plan to put gas in the car tonight before you worry tomorrow? If you are anxious about something big like death, can you plan out some amazing things you are going to do in life and work on those? What is yours? What is your plan? Write it down.

DAY TWENTY

Resting In His Presence

Read: *"God is our refuge and strength, A very present help in trouble. Therefore, we will not fear" Psalm 46:1-2*

Reflect

When writing this, my daughter, who was eight years old at the time, and my son, who was seven, locked themselves in the back room of our business located in the local mall. They were looking for me, but the door refused to open from the inside for them. Of course, panic set in as they tried to call for help and open the door. My daughter's instinct was to break her way out after realizing no one heard them crying out for help. She picked up the nearest thing, something that looked like a baseball bat, and swung it at the door. Great instinct, but what she picked was a fluorescent light. It shattered everywhere.

As you can imagine, this made the stakes even higher. Now they were stuck, shoes off, with broken glass all over the floor. Whatever anxiety was present before, it transformed itself into complete fear. Needless to say, they were in trouble.

This psalm encourages us to rest in God's presence. After reminding us of His character and posture towards His people ("refuge… strength… very present help"), the psalmist applies what one author calls the logic of faith:

If God is all of these things, and He is with us, there is no logical reason to fear, even in the worst circumstances.

The psalmist focuses entirely on God's character and provision. He does not even mention his need. His focus is strictly on who God is and what He is able to do for His people.

He is a safe place. He is the one who makes us strong and bold to face challenges. He is constantly present and active in helping us, not passive or distant.

Everything in the psalm flows out of God's active presence. Because God is in the midst of Jerusalem, she is immovable (v. 5). Because God is with His people, He is their fortress (v. 7). Because God is present, He makes wars cease and shatters the implements of warfare (vv.8-9). We can be still and know that He really is God (v. 10).

The psalm closes with a reaffirmation of God's presence manifested as protection. "The LORD of hosts is with us; the God of Jacob is our refuge" (v. 11). God is immediately, personally, and actively present with His people as their impregnable fortress, their unconquerable safe place in the midst of terror.

But tell that to my daughter, who was in panic mode and felt the need to save her brother as well. Luckily a customer heard their cries and opened the door for them. Without delay, they rushed to my office, where they knew I would eventually be. After being told by the customer what happened, I walked in to find my daughter trying to hide her tears. Before I could ask if she was okay, she hugged me and felt peace.

When we take the time to be still before God, we open ourselves up to His presence and His peace. In His presence, we can find comfort and strength, guidance and direction, and the assurance that He is with us always.

Because God is with us, we can be strong. He will act as our place of refuge, as our Deliverer, and as our Strength on the day of battle. Whatever our need is, God's personal presence promises to meet them.

We must look to Him and be consumed by confidence in His ability and not be swayed by our fears, no matter how big they may be.

Journal

- Do you really believe that God's presence logically eliminates the "need" to be afraid? Why or why not?

- How does the fact that the psalmist focuses entirely on God's character and presence change the amount of attention and focus we should give to our fears?

- Think deeply about what it means for God to be your refuge. How does this apply to the things that make you afraid? Be as specific as possible.

Act

We are going to do something a little different. Write your own prayer of intention below as the Lord directs you. Will you choose to trust God's presence and ability and not be swayed by fear? The prayer should answer this question and explain why you will not be swayed. Concentrate on God's character to always be there for you instead of what you can do, not to be afraid. Make it just like the prayers written in this book. Then pray it with all your heart.

Prayer

Pray your own prayer here.

DAY TWENTY-ONE

Never Alone

Read: *"Be strong and of good courage, do not fear nor be afraid of them; for the Lord your God, He is the One who goes with you. He will not leave you nor forsake you." Deuteronomy 31:6*

Reflect

The Scripture promises you that God will always be with you through this life and beyond.

One of the biggest misconceptions about the Bible is that people think there is a verse that says, *"God will never give us anything we can't handle."* No such verse exists. Nowhere in the Bible will you find that promise. The Bible verse people may be referring to is about temptation. God will never tempt us more than we can bear, can be found in 1 Corinthians 10:13.

"No temptation has overtaken you except such as is common to man; but God is faithful, who will not allow you to be tempted beyond what you are able, but with the temptation will also make the way of escape, that you may be able to bear it."

Although God will not allow us to be tempted beyond what we can bear, that doesn't mean he promised things wouldn't happen to us that we can't bear. Things do happen that are too much for us. He does, however, promise to be there with us.

Even in the darkest of circumstances, the Lord is still present. Jesus said,

> *"Lo, I am with you always, even unto the end of the world..."*
> *Matthew 28:20.*

This promise is echoed throughout the Bible and serves as a reminder to you today that God is always with you, even in your loneliest moments. Even in your hardest moments. Even in those moments that are unbearable. He is there.

And Jesus also promises in John 14:18,

> *"I will not leave you comfortless: I will come to you."*

Does that encourage you? There will never be a single minute of your life when you are alone. God is always with you, always on your side, always guiding you, always protecting you.

There may be times when you feel like you're alone, but you're not. Throughout the Bible, God is often described as a shepherd. Shepherds always keep a close watch over their sheep.

They ensure that the sheep are fed and protected. If a wild animal approaches, the shepherd will fight the animal and drive it off.

God cares for you similarly, constantly watching over you and fighting on your behalf. God won't fail you. God won't forsake you. God won't leave you. When you feel anxious, take comfort in God's constant presence in your life.

Journal

- How does it encourage you that God will never leave you?

- What does it mean that God is your shepherd?

- How does it change your perspective on past events knowing that God was with you every step?

- What Bible verses can you turn to when you feel alone?

Pray

Father, thank you that you will never leave me or forsake me, regardless of what I'm going through -- whether I'm having a good day or bad. You're always by my side and will sustain me even in the toughest times.

Help me to rest in your constant presence. Your presence is my peace. Your presence is my joy. Your presence is my hope. When I feel weighed down by worry and anxious thoughts, I take comfort in knowing that you are always with me.

Forgive me for the times when I haven't taken refuge in your presence, for the times when I've ignored prayer or your Word. Assist me in seeking refuge in you when I experience anxiety, so that I may find solace in the peace that you provide without any delay. In Jesus' name, amen.

Act

Think of a time you've felt the most alone. Maybe you've even felt alone even when people are around you. But you've felt so alone you are in despair. You felt that you couldn't bear it any longer. The thought of this even brings on anxiety and fear. It could be now or a time in your past. Take some time to close your eyes and think about this, then without hesitation, write for 3 minutes straight. The only thing you are allowed to write is thanks to God that he was/is with you in this time of loneliness and despair. Praise Him. 3 minutes. Go.

DAY TWENTY-TWO

Anxiety Is A Liar

Read: *"Which of you by taking thought can add one cubit unto his stature?" Matthew 6:27*

Reflect

Anxiety and worry are kind of silly when you think about it. Being obsessed with anxious thoughts will not help you in any way whatsoever. That's the lie of anxiety. It tells you lies about the future and then makes you think about them constantly.

As you confront the very things that make you anxious, you're like a soldier attacking an unseen enemy. The problem with the unseen is that you forget that it's there! Your "spiritual eyes" must be opened.

Imagine for a moment that anxiety (fear) is a person.

This person wants to keep you unsettled, so he starts whispering things into your heart all the time, things that are untrue. This enemy tells you that bad things are going to happen. The fact that these things won't happen doesn't matter. This adversary only wants you to expend tons of energy thinking about these things.

And if you pay close attention, you will probably notice that most of your anxious thoughts don't include God in the picture. You're imagining a future where God is not present to help you.

So, the next time anxious thoughts cloud your thinking and tempt you to leave God out of the picture, remember this vivid concept of a lying foe who hates you.

And the truth is, the devil really does want you to be so preoccupied with worry that you forget about God. The more time you spend worrying, the less time you spend praying, loving others, and trusting God.

Journal

- What are some of the "lies" anxiety has told you?

- What Bible verses can you use to dispel those lies?

- What practices or daily habits do you think would help arm or prepare you to battle anxious thoughts?

- How would it change your life if you spent less time worrying and more time trusting God?

Pray

Father, forgive me for all the time I have wasted worrying. Forgive me for believing the lies of anxiety. Forgive me for listening to anxiety rather than the promises you make in the Bible.

By your power, help me to spend more time thinking about you and all the ways you bless me rather than my anxiety. Help me to fix my gaze on you, not being distracted by anxiety but constantly trusting you instead.

I know that anxiety is a liar and that you always tell the truth. When I feel anxious and worried, help me to tune out the lies and focus all my thoughts and energy on your wonderful truths. Thank you for loving and being with me even when I'm worried. In Jesus' Name, amen.

Act

On your phone or computer, Google God's Soldier and click on images. Find an image that you like and make that your screensaver, desktop picture, or lock screen picture. This is a reminder that this picture represents you fighting anxiety and fear. Never forget that you are fighting for a better, anxiety-free, fearless, peaceful life!

DAY TWENTY-THREE

Trusting In God To Change You

Read: "Now unto him that is able to do exceeding abundantly above all that we ask or think, according to the power that worketh in us"
Ephesians 3:20

Reflect

If you have struggled with fear and anxiety for a long time, you might be tempted to think that you'll never make any progress.

If you were the one ultimately responsible for making all the changes, you would have reason to be discouraged.

But the good news is that God is the one who can change us.

He conquered fear and death, so God certainly has the ability to transform you and manage your anxious thoughts! He also loves you more than you can possibly imagine.

Take another look at our verse. It says God is able to do so much more abundantly above all that we could ever ask for or think can be possible. How? Because it's not according to our power to do it, it's according to the power that works in us. The power He put there by the Holy Spirit.

God's power is at work in you! He can do more than you could possibly think, ask, or imagine. Imagine living a life free from anxiety. God can do even more than that. He can set you free from anxiety and worry in ways that you never thought were possible. Your

Father in heaven knows the plans He has for you, and those plans are good ones. Jeremiah 29:11 says,

> *"For I know the thoughts that I think toward you, saith the Lord, thoughts of peace, and not of evil, to give you an expected end."*

God has plans of peace for you. Plans of rest. Good plans that are full of blessings. Peace in times of trouble is a process of growth. Some days will be easier than others, but you have a strong ally in your fight against anxiety.

These words written by hymn writer - Stuart Townend capture the glorious present and future reality your loving Father has for you:

No guilt in life, no fear in death,

This is the power of Christ in me.

From life's first cry to final breath,

Jesus commands my destiny.

No power of hell, no scheme of man,

Can ever pluck me from His hand.

Till He returns or calls me home

Here in the power of Christ I'll stand.

We may struggle with fear and anxiety now, but as we ask God for help, He will transform us. Now that's some good news!

Journal

- How can trust in God help you to make positive changes in your life?

- What are some common challenges people face when trying to trust God to change them?

- How can prayer and meditation help you to trust in God to change you?

- How can trusting God to change you bring peace and fulfill-ment to your life?

Pray

Lord, please help me to put everything I've learned into action. Help me to rely on you in every aspect of my life. Help me to realize that you are with me always and are always working on my behalf. Teach me to be grateful for all you have already done and given me, and grant me the peace of Christ that is beyond all comprehension. Guard my heart and my mind. In Jesus' name, Amen!

Act

Take out that envelope we created when we first began this journey. Open it. Read it. You committed to completing this program. You made it! You never gave up! Did you take action every day?

If you did, then there should have been some significant change in your life. You wrote down what you thought you would look like at the end of this program. Were you right? Did you see a change? Was it better than you thought, or do you think you need more work? Remember, this whole program is a process. Don't be anxious if you feel you haven't made the strides you wish you had. The next chapter is for you! God is with you. See you tomorrow for our final chapter and action.

DAY TWENTY-FOUR

It's A Process

Read: *"The thief does not come except to steal, and to kill, and to destroy. I have come that they may have life, and that they may have it more abundantly." John 10:10*

Reflect

God desires abundant life for His people. This includes freedom from fear. Why? Because our Redeemer, Jesus Christ, reverses everything that sin has brought into our lives. He does not want you to walk in fear but to be confident in His ability to protect, uphold, bless, establish, and vindicate you.

Freedom from anxiety and fear is a process, particularly if you have habitually given in to anxious thoughts and fear! Since it took a significant amount of time to develop these negative habits, it will require considerable time and effort to undo and replace them with positive ones.

Don't be discouraged if you find yourself still feeling anxiety or fear after completing this program. Continue to choose to trust what God says about you, about Himself, and about His purposes. As you make choices of faith, they build up over time into a new way of life.

God is merciful. Do not allow your fearfulness to make you shrink away from God in shame. Come to Him boldly in Christ, owning your weaknesses and inviting His help and enablement by His Spirit. God takes pleasure in delivering you from difficulties and demonstrating his unwavering loyalty to you time after time! Never give up hope that you will be set free.

The first step to liberty from any life-dominating habit or bondage is to believe God can set you free. Don't ever lose that! Believing you cannot change or that your life can't be different will only keep you in chains. Choosing to trust God's ability to set you free is vitally important.

Get to know your God. The more you know Him, the more you will trust Him, and the more you trust Him, the more transformation will take place in your life.

If you need to, when you are done with the last pages of this book, close it, pray, and open it right back up again to page one and take the program again. Take all the actions over again every day! It takes action to make a change! Choose, Read, Reflect, Journal, Pray, and Act. See you again soon!

Journal

- Are there areas where you still question His goodness or desire to help you? Be specific.

- What is the most important or most helpful thing you have learned from this program?

- How, if at all, have your anxieties and fears lessened after this deep dive into God's desire for you to be free from fear?

- Do you have real hope that God can set you free from fear? What is the one thing that most inspired this hope in you?

Pray

Lord, thank you for being with me as I continue my journey to overcome anxiety and fear. I know you are with me through it all. I've learned that you never leave my side, even in the hardest times, providing me with strength and courage. I know you are with me through this process. Please give me the wisdom and clarity to see the path ahead clearly, and the patience and perseverance to stay the course, even when it feels difficult.

Bestow upon me the serenity of mind that stems from the recognition that you are the one in charge, and irrespective of the circumstances that may arise, all things will eventually come together for my benefit since you have summoned me according to your purpose. Help me to trust in Your plan for my life, even when it feels scary or uncertain.

Give me the courage to go through this program again so that I can continue to grow. In Jesus' Name. Amen.

Act

Be free from Anxiety & Fear. Choose an action. Go back to the beginning of this book or get your Bible out and remember to Read, Reflect, Journal, Pray and Act!

ABOUT THE AUTHOR

Wally De La Fuente

"And whatever you do, do it heartily, as to the Lord and not to men, knowing that from the Lord you will receive the reward of the inheritance; for[a] you serve the Lord Christ." Colossians 3:23–24

Wally De La Fuente has been a Commissioned Pastor and a church planter for the Reformed Church in America with a Master of Theological Studies. He has worked in various full time church positions in the past such as Worship Leader and Video Director, and Pastor. He currently works for Multiplication Network as the Center for Innovation and Technology Specialist where he designed and implemented an online training platform to assist in the planting of churches around the world. Wally also owns businesses as an entrepreneur and has written other books such as Come To Your Senses, an in-depth study into the parable of the Lost Son; and the upcoming 90 Day Disciples Program, Compound Discipleship books and a Pastoral Entrepreneurship Program. He is married with children.

Milton Keynes UK
Ingram Content Group UK Ltd.
UKHW020059080823
426465UK00009B/37